The Matrix of Splendor

Also by Don C. Nix

The Matrix of Splendor

Reaching Toward the Heart of the Cosmos

by Don C. Nix, J.D., Ph.D.

iUniverse, Inc.
New York   Bloomington

The Matrix of Splendor
Reaching Toward the Heart of the Cosmos

iUniverse books may be ordered through booksellers or by contacting:

iUniverse
1663 Liberty Drive
Bloomington, IN 47403
www.iuniverse.com
1-800-Authors (1-800-288-4677)

ISBN: 978-1-4502-5808-1 (sc)
ISBN: 978-1-4502-5809-8 (ebook)

Printed in the United States of America

iUniverse rev. date: 09/10/2010

Dedication

To Faisel Muqaddam, my teacher and friend for 20 years now. I found you when I was in trouble, in emotional disintegration, and your instruction and care was life-changing for me. You took my hand and gently guided me from despair and emptiness back to meaning, depth and Being. Perhaps you guided me back to life. You fill a room with your heart, and it was exactly what I needed for healing. Thank you for your concern and attention to me all these years, for your incomparable visionary consciousness, and for your great humanity. I'm only one of countless people you have led back into contact with Being and a richer, deeper life. With great affection and appreciation.

Don C. Nix
Sonoma, CA
August 2010

Contents

Introduction

We are desperate for Spirit while it is pouring Itself upon us. We are caught in a mistake of history that tells us, through the predominance of our science, that we live in a dead and empty Cosmos. When we believe this, it leaves us desperate, in despair, and frantic for some meaning in our lives. Modern man in modern Western culture is searching for the philosopher's stone of happiness, the one thing that will make life not only tolerable but wonderful. Many among us, echoing the materialistic bent of science, have landed on money, goods and fame as the crucial requirements. However, a quick look at the rich and famous among us reveals that they are not particularly happy. Indeed, many of them seem to exist in absolute misery. Perhaps it is because they achieved what they were told would do the trick, and it made absolutely no difference. They are still confronting emptiness.

What can change our inner dynamics is the re-introduction of Being into our framework. If we can integrate the truth that the Cosmos is a living, conscious, mysterious Field that has the peculiar power to throw up worlds and populate them, and that we are graced to simply be alive inside It, to experience this miraculous Field, suddenly the emptiness yields to fullness. The deadness is replaced by pure Livingness. We are suddenly part of something magnificent, so vast, powerful and beautiful that it stuns us with wonder. Our spirits lift—permanently. We are back home where we belong, back inside the Matrix of Splendor.

1

I am something magnificent.
I have roots in the
Matrix of Splendor.
I am thrown up,
in an act of grace,
from the depths of Cosmic Life.
I am the part of Earth
that walks around on itself.
I am the unfolding embodiment
of the Eternal One.
I am Mystery's child,
now awake and aware,
now stunned into silent wonder.

2

I don't have time for trivia.
The clock is ticking.
My life is unfolding.
My life's hourglass
is dropping its sand.
I am pushed from the depths
to say my piece
and speak my truth,
right now.
My voice is both me
and greater than me.
I am laced with intent Sublime.
When I speak what I see
it's both me and not me.
The Cosmos speaks
one mouth at a time.

3

If you had infinite power
and creativity was your game,
and if you were invisible
and if you had no name,
what would you choose
to do with yourself
to pass your infinite life?
Why not make worlds of drama,
of joy and pain and strife?
Why not make beings of sentience
and give them lessons to learn?
Why not throw worlds into motion,
pit light against dark endlessly?
Why not craft dramas of meaning
and see how they play themselves out?
At the end of the game,
when the outcomes are clear,
return it all whence it came.
With a laugh you dissolve it
all back into space,
all that exaltation, fear and pain.

4

All this sound and light show,
all this cavalcade of wonders,
all this blazing fireworks burst
will eventually go black.
We are caught in a whirling dance
of changing form in motion.
We cannot fathom it.
It is full of threads
of joy and pain and strife.
Relax and enjoy the ride.
This is what's called life.

5

An inner door opens
and I am lifted suddenly,
and disarmingly,
out of my little self.
I draw near
to the door's dark
and to the silent
and fecund Presence
that hovers just inside it.
As I draw near
I am flooded with the gifts
of Its nature—
joy, depth, sacredness,
insight, vastness, livingness.
My nervous system
lights up with delight,
and I become one
with the Cosmos.

6

The world is a phantom
unfolding itself,
relentlessly
and eternally,
into the new and unknown.
We're brought on board,
miraculously
and temporarily,
to act our part
and read our lines
and push the play
to a conclusion
that never comes.

7

I cannot tell you
what the next second
will bring.
I'm not in control here.
I have no rudder
to inflect my life.
I cannot determine
my course.
I'm in the grip
of Something
so vast
and so complex
and so powerful
that my only choice
is to relax
and surrender,
and enjoy the ride
while it lasts.

8

Who is this miracle
sitting in this chair,
with a sensitized pool,
perceiving and interacting
with a restless,
churning world.
I'm awake.
I'm aware.
I'm unfolding my little self
and becoming something new.
I watch the panorama
from my privileged place,
as the future hoves breathlessly
into view.

9

Pull me into Your Cosmic embrace.
Usher me through the stars.
Shed the warmth of Your heart
upon my face.
Open me to Your joy.
Flow Your belonging through me.
Let me see infinity.
Give me Your gifts abundant
before I'm whisked from the earth
and dissolved
in Your limitless
Cosmic Sea.

10

Pour your essence into the world.
Be who you were born to be.
Find yourself in the chaos and whirl
and blow through your limits now.
Carve out your depths to the Sacred.
Broaden your mind to the Void.
See through the surface
skin of the world
to the shimmering Light beneath.

11

The I that is walking the earth
is a clever and adept imposter,
a charlatan,
a con-man,
a defrauder,
devoted to having his needs met
and looking good
and increasing his status.
He approaches the world
as a bank to be robbed,
not as a Wholeness
of Wonder.
Surely,
somewhere in this me,
a greater soul resides,
awake to the depths,
and sacredness,
and mystery,
and eternity.
Where can I meet that man?

12

I look out into the world.
Vast beauty and
vast pain
in equal proportions.
I try to understand.
I step into the depths,
searching,
searching,
for the one insight
that will give it all
some sense.
The Cosmos rebuffs me.
I slam against a wall.
I begin to suspect that
with this brain,
in this state of evolution,
I will not be able
to see it all.

13

We stand on the shoulders
of those who have gone before.
Like us,
they were frightened
and struggling.
Like us,
they tried to understand.
Like us,
They looked at the sparkling stars
and the vastness of Living Space,
and felt their hearts
bursting in wonder
to be in this sacred place.

14

My heart fills up
and overflows.
Tears spill.
I burst my bounds.
I'm touched by Something
deep and rich
and quite beyond my kin.
I bloom inside
with gratitude
to see this dream I'm in.

15

Before me lies the Abyss.
I peer into its depths.
The darkness overwhelms me.
The fear constricts my heart.
What if that Void is living?
What if It's loving me?
What if I could see
the whole of things,
and realize the miracle
it is to be?

16

We've lost our way.
Our compass is gone.
We're stumbling
across the earth.
We're searching
for the way back home,
trying to recover
our birth.
We thought that
we created life
and held things
all together.
But now we find
we're helpless,
and clueless,
and useless,
to control the earth
to control the weather.
The Cosmos is
just reminding us
from whence we came.
It's putting us back
in our proper place.
It's telling us
that although we boast,
we're pawns in
the Cosmic game.

17

Vast Livingness.
Deep Mind.
A shimmering,
gossamer Sea.
We buy our shoes
and cook our food
without a thought
for these.
We live our lives
in one dimension,
flat and filled with fear,
while out beyond,
in every direction,
lies the spectrum
of Living Infinity.

18

Wake up!
Wake up!
Come and
join the spectacular show.
The bands are playing.
The clowns are clowning,
The twirlers are throwing
batons in the air.
The suns are bursting.
The planets are swinging.
The world is unfolding
its drama there.
Wake up to the wonder
and join the parade.
It's now or never.
Wake up!
Wake up!

19

I am touched by miracle
as I sit by the morning fire.
My mind expands.
My edges push out.
I fall into
a well of wonder.
The sun is coming.
The earth is waking.
The dance is about to resume.
Here in my house,
in my little life,
Something
is opening
my heart.

20

Why can't I see You
as you work Your magic?
Why can't I get
just a glimpse?
I can feel You
in my heart and cells,
but I'd like to connect
with my eyes.
Could it be that
there is nothing to see?
Are You just a
Miraculous Space,
Your talent
for creating stars and worlds
the same Force
that is throwing up me?

21

I want to push deeper.
I want to see the truth.
I want to be
aware and awake
to the miracle that is me.
I want to touch
the core of the Cosmos,
and swim in the waters
of Life.
Submerge me
and engulf me,
now,
give me moments
of ecstasy.

22

The currents of life
are moving.
Things are not standing still.
Our earth is spinning
through blackest night,
dancing passionately
with the sun.
Below the crust
of what we see,
potential gathers itself.
Soon it will burst
through the surface of life
and become our reality.

23

A pulse is pounding
beneath the world,
beating in regular time,
and as it strikes
its deepest note,
we enter the Sublime.
We are not the point here.
Our miracle is one of many.
The Field of mysterious energy,
the Sea of Life beneath,
is the source of our intensity,
the core of our reality.
Fall on your knees
in wonder,
bow your head in awe.
Open your eyes
to see the Real,
and melt into the Mystery.

24

Dawn breaks.
Earth spins.
Birds wake.
Day begins.
Life rouses itself
from slumber.
The future pushes
to emerge.
We watch
from our perch,
wondrous and expectant,
as the Cosmos unfolds Itself.

25

I inhabit my body
like an old overcoat,
familiar and frayed,
softened by years of wear.
I rarely pause to see it,
put it squarely in my gaze.
But now,
in this moment of quiet,
I turn toward its qualities.
Thank you for your loyalty.
Thank you for your zeal.
Thank you for your effort
in carrying me through the decades.
I see you're tiring now.
You're flagging in the race.
In moments you are unsteady.
It's hard to hold your place.
Thank you for trying so hard,
and for bearing the burden so long,
Thank you for not complaining
and thank you for serving me so well.

26

The middle of night.
I'm wide awake.
The earth is silent and still.
The stars are there,
above the roof,
shining their life away.
I'm pushed from within
to get up and do,
but the house is asleep
and there's nothing to view.
Perhaps this is also life,
with a value all its own.
I am,
after all,
awake and aware,
and charge bubbles through
my limbs.
I will lie here peacefully
and contemplate
how it feels to be,
and just how it feels,
in this moment of night
to be the little me.
I'll use this quiet
in the depth of night
to restore my sanity.

27

I yearn.
I reach.
I grasp for You,
but there seems to be nothing there.
I cannot see You
with my eyes,
or touch You
with my hands.
I long to see
this Cosmic Sea
that surrounds
and nourishes me.
But It is much too subtle,
beyond the reach
of animal sense.
I must see You with
my inner eye.
I must hear You with
my inner ear.
I must develop the art
of touching You
with the radar
of my heart.

28

I both am and am not
the Cosmos.
It depends
on your point of view.
I'm both inside and outside
the Living Field.
I'm both joined at the hip
with the vastness of Life,
and living the separate me.
It's a matter of perspective.
There are many levels here.
The self that I feel
when I walk the earth
results from where I see.
I can go in a flash
from this separate self
to a particle in
the Cosmic Sea.

29

The night is soft and lovely.
Earth stills
and rests
and waits.
The frantic dance
is slowed now.
Distractions now are few.
Beneath the velvet blackness
a Vastness can be felt,
a living, conscious Presence
comes slowly into view.
I feel It in the silence.
I feel It in the dark.
My heart wakes up and reaches.
I want to touch Its grace.
My cells are filled with yearning
to feel Its arms,
to see Its face,
but I know
in this moment of wanting
that this cannot possibly be.
This Presence that
I long to clasp
is only Living Space.

30

Here comes the morning light.
As I sit by the fire,
all lost in my dreams,
the earth is dancing its way
to day.
Radiance is returning.
How many times
in the course of my years
have I watched
the return of the Light?
How many times
has my heart been renewed
when I was lost in my fears?
Something is there
renewing me.
Something is beating my heart.
Something is
somehow in this Light
that is coming now
as I watch from my chair,
wonder-struck, breathlessly.

31

I look through eyes of wonder.
There is radiance in all that I view.
The world is a shifting kaleidoscope,
ever changing,
ever fresh,
ever new.
The Cosmos does not repeat Itself.
Invention is Its name.
It effortlessly unfolds Its wealth,
perfectly harmonious,
perfectly collated,
perfectly balanced,
perfectly blooming Itself
into new life.

32

Enter my aging heart.
Resurrect my worn-out cells.
Give me a moment
of newness.
Give me a fresh, new start.
I still have things to explore.
I still have miles to go.
I'm still held breathless
in wonder
at the miracle of this show.

33

Futility is the enemy.
It lurks there in the night.
What if my life
has made no difference?
What if I'm irrelevant?
I've lived to have
some meaning.
I pursue it even now.
I wanted to make a difference
but I didn't know exactly how.

34

I've always run
from emptiness.
I was scared
of having space.
I filled my life
up to the brim,
in motion,
whirling,
juggling,
dancing
a St. Vitus dance.
What if that Space
is living?
What if It's
seeking me?
Have I pushed away
from the sacred Divine
in my quest to be
totally free?

35

In some way
I've been guided.
I'm not a free agent here.
It's only as I look back
that the pattern
becomes more clear.
My life has been a convergence.
Complexity is its name.
I'm a collection of finely
woven threads,
and meanings,
and influences,
and surprises,
in the tapestry
of this life.

36

Just before dawn
the world is blue
and the world is silent and still.
I listen and I watch
as the future comes gliding
over the hill.
The Unseen is unfolding.
I feel Its power now
as It makes the world,
and changes the world
and brings Itself into view.

37

I am caught in a web
of miracle.
I have been
since my birth.
It's here now
all around me,
dancing,
throbbing,
pulsing with life,
metamorphosing.
It's the matrix
that we live in.
We call it Planet Earth.

38

I fall to my knees
in wonder
as I view
the miraculous Earth.
Life comes,
life goes,
life blooms,
and withers
and replenishes itself,
and recreates itself.
Just open your eyes
to see it
and feel it
with your cells.
We are living inside
of strangeness.
It's always there
with us,
but we close our eyes
to wonder.
We're asleep to miracle now.

39

In a sea of darkness
particles float,
waiting for the Touch.
One by one
they light up.
Novelty arrives.
Consciousness expands.
New light flashes.
Chance begins.
The dark sea is illumined now.
The light is growing bright.
We're subsumed
in brilliant radiance
as we press forward
into an unknown dawn.

40

Sometimes,
without any warning,
I merge with the
grass and the trees.
I lose myself
and my little concerns
and become
the vast blue sky.
I wait for
these precious moments,
when the walls of my self
go down.
I yearn to be part
of the Big Life,
to be swept
into miracle.

41

Change involves death.
The Buddha saw it clearly.
The way things are must die,
so the future can arrive.
We don't much like
this part of life.
We'd rather turn our heads.
We'd like to continue
the good parts
and avoid the passing forms.
But the Cosmos has Its nature.
It's relentless and impartial
with Its processes of change.
The things we love will go.
We are moved through
the cycle of our little lives
until,
battered and exhausted,
and wiser,
we are ready to go home.

42

What should I do with myself
in the time I have left on Earth?
With a world in total chaos,
should I pitch in and help?
How much could I accomplish?
What difference would I make?
The needs are over-whelming.
The agonies are real.
We have a world of pain here
but is it up to me?
Perhaps my course is other.
Withdrawal is its name.
If I apply myself
to evolving myself,
and to sensing the Cosmic Other,
perhaps this could be my game.
Perhaps it's not up to me.
The Cosmos shaped me
and put me here.
It made me a certain way.
Perhaps I should
search Its instructions
on what to do today.

43

I seem to be invisible.
I leave no footprint in the world.
I live my little life
in my own little way,
quite unnoticed,
quite unseen.
Perhaps it's true
of all of us.
Our impact here is brief,
a splashing wave
in a vast, vast Sea,
now here, now gone,
now vanished forevermore.
The impulse to be seen
is chimera.
Perhaps it's enough
to just be.

44

Something paints my paintings.
Something writes my poems.
An impulse within
is pushing me
to make something new and fine.
What is this mysterious push
that moves me through my life
and impels my creativity,
that enlists me now,
in my own little way,
to participate in the shaping of
an emerging, marvelous world?

45

We die many times in our life.
We are reborn many times too.
Life is an on-going
sacrificial event,
a sacrament of death,
and rebirth,
and annihilation,
and transcendance.
We are recreated
not only year to year
but moment to moment,
aligned always toward
the future,
traveling an arc
that ends in Mystery.

46

The sun comes sailing
over the hill,
bringing the future,
bringing my life.
The earth is eagerly waiting now,
for its touch,
for its warmth,
for its infinite nourishment.
We live in bursts of sunlight,
that are sent our way
by a burning star
that is our heart,
that is our food,
that is our living source.

47

Emptiness is an illusion.
It doesn't really exist.
We are swimming
in a Sea of Meaning.
We are held
by a Cosmic Force.
Wake up to Reality's dancing.
Wake up to the Miracles that be.
Plunge into the Fullness
around you.
Submerge yourself in the Cosmic Sea.

48

When I am near to Being
my spirits lift,
the Cosmos is full,
I can see beyond myself.
My heart is irrigated
by the gifts of the Sublime—
freshness,
hope,
joy,
sacredness,
depth.
I want to learn
to live here.
I'm struggling to make it so.
But I know that
I'm still incomplete,
and I have miles to go.

49

My heart expands
in morning light,
as I touch the
Living Dawn.
New life is flooding
from the Sun,
the future is coming on.
I open to its mystery.
I'm poised here in my chair,
expectant,
hopeful,
fearful,
breathless,
alive and in Its care.

50

The poem is already there.
My job is to get out of the way.
Like a bubble from
beneath the sea,
the poem rises,
already complete,
with meaning or not,
it is already what it will be.
It comes from the depths
of the Living Sea
far, far beyond the little me.

51

The trash truck rumbles.
The day begins.
Potential opens its door.
I look to the future
to save my life,
for sustenance
and more.
I need to live in the present,
the present that is always here,
the present that glides seamlessly
from moment to following moment.
The past is gone forever.
The future has not yet arrived.
I must live my life
in the Eternal Now.
Life unfolds Itself right here.

52

My consciousness is magical,
a miracle behind my eyes,
shimmering,
radiant,
collating,
understanding,
moving me through my life.
We rarely stop to notice
this marvel that we have,
that's there within us every day,
upon which everything depends.
We miss its magic
and live in flatness.
Blind and dumb,
We pass right by
this stunning, miraculous land.

53

The world turns
and my heart yearns
for the touch
of Living Space.
Take me to
the depths of Life.
Touch me with
Your wonder.
Open my heart
to Vastness.
Lift me out
of this limited place.

54

When I see the world
from my heart,
I am filled
with the wonder of it.
Life blooms in the space
all around.
The Cosmos is bursting
to become.
I am open to the miracle
that it is to just be me.
For a while I can walk the earth,
I can wake to Reality.
I can stroll through the Cosmos
and taste Its delights,
in wonder at all that I see.

55

Dawn breaks.
The stars wink out.
The earth is spinning
its way through space.
The sand in the hourglass
of my life
keeps dropping,
dropping,
dropping.
If I'm ever going
to wake up,
I'd better do it now.
I'm trying my best
to push out my edges
but I don't know exactly how.

56

Something is pushing me
through my life.
I can feel It in my depths.
I am being unfolded
in harmonious complexity,
here tugged,
there nudged,
on paths I never knew existed.
I open to it now.
I put myself in Your hands.
Do with me what you will.
Your Mystery is so much
greater than me.
I wait for Your next revelation.

57

I stand at the edge
of the Cosmos.
I gaze at the blackness of space.
I see the stars
in their brilliance,
shining and winking in place.
I am graced to be
consciously witnessing this.
I'm the child of royalty here.
I'm a point of light
in this infinite night.
Truly, what is there to fear?

58

Give me a moment of splendor.
Open my little self.
Bloom my heart into a great thing.
Empty my mind and fire my nerves,
so that I may feel Your Life.
Course Yourself through my body.
Fill me with Your truth.
I'm in my chair,
waiting,
for Your stunning, miraculous touch.

59

What is it that
I'm supposed to do
in this time
when the world's gone wrong?
I look out on life
with a sinking heart.
I see war
and pain
and strife.
Perhaps my view is partial.
Perhaps I cannot see
the way the Lifeforce
is unfolding Itself,
the way things are meant to be.
I know that Whirl is not King here.
I know that deep order prevails.
I know that beneath
the suffering
lies a shimmering, life-filled Sea.

60

Can I find ways to deepen,
to touch the Living Mystery?
Can I be trained to open
my cells to the Sublime?
Can I learn to clear and empty
this agitated mind?
Can I burst through my bounds
and open my heart
to That beyond space and time?

61

Why was I sent here
to walk the earth
and what am I
supposed to do?
What is the purpose
for which I came?
How should I fit myself
into the skein
of this mysterious,
unfolding game?
The weaving is vast.
The pattern is hidden.
The Cosmos does not tip Its hand.
We dance our dance.
We live our lives
without guide or map
to this strange land.

62

Meaning is at the heart of things.
We search and search to find it.
We feel it can be,
and we sometimes see,
how things fit all together.
But most of the time
we search in vain
for the meaning beneath the pain.
We keep on looking
and keep on living,
without knowing how or why.
We're sent here from space
to this lovely place,
to play this mysterious
and unknown game.

63

I'm here,
I'm aware,
I'm expectant.
I'm ready to give my all.
Just touch me,
and use me,
and move me.
I'm waiting for your call.

64

How will I know
when I'm moved by You?
What should I look for now?
I want to make
my contribution.
I want to give
my gift.
I cannot see
what I'm meant to be
in Your vast and complex
unfolding plan.
The world looms out before me.
I know that I have
a part to play.
I offer myself,
I submit myself
to be used as you wish today.

65

I dip myself into Your depths.
I touch Your electric Life.
I open myself,
and my cells and my heart,
to Your ceaseless bountiful gifts.
Radiance is flowing through me.
Something is firing my mind.
In this moment of bliss
I am borne away,
the shadow of grief
left behind.

66

I swim in the sea of Your goodness.
I am warmed by the fires of Your heart.
I am stunned by the gifts
that You pour upon me,
as I sit in my chair
at this dawning of day.
Your radiance flares brightly around me.
My heart swings wide and open.
and I'm thrilled,
as I hoped to be,
from the depths of your infinite Vastness,
with the joy of
Your shimmering Cosmic Sea.

67

Poised on the brink
of the moment to come,
I open myself
to what I will be.
I see that I have
my preferences.
I see that I want control.
But the plan of the Sea
is so far beyond me
that my only course
is surrender.

68

I search for my place
in the order of things.
I would like it to be
really grand.
But I fear that I'm small,
not important at all,
and, in any case, transient
and on the way out.
Perhaps I am searching for value
in a place that it does not exist.
To be born on this earth,
to be conscious,
to have walked as a man
through the Cosmos,
to be graced with the gifts
of this life and this mind,
this is value,
this is important.
In this moment I see
value greater than me.
I am part of the Cosmic design.

69

I touch the Body Electric.
My nerves and my mind light up.
I am filled
with the will
of a Presence,
so powerful
and yet so subtle.
I can feel You in my cells.
I can sense You in the room.
I touch You with
my filling heart,
as Your Presence makes me bloom.

70

How paltry are my little poems.
How insignificant.
I reach into
and try to view
the Presence that hovers
beneath all forms.
I'm moved to try to craft it
in images and in words,
but the impulse may be misguided.
My Subject is so very vast,
and alive,
and conscious,
and mysterious,
and deep,
and intangible,
and radiating miraculous qualities.
My efforts to try
to bring It in view,
are clumsy and small,
but the best I can do.

71

I am the Cosmos walking.
So are you.
We are only one thing
though we seem to be two.
Our senses are deceiving.
We cannot see the Deep.
We live our lives on the surface,
restless,
dissatisfied,
struggling,
threatened.
We yearn for depth and meaning,
but we don't know where to look.
We are still being unfolded.
Give us time.
Give us time.

72

Life courses through me,
and renews me,
and sustains me now on this planet
for just this briefest time.
I want to wake up
and see and revel
in the riches cascading upon me.
I want to wake up
and fully see
the unfolding miracle
that is my body,
that is my mind,
that is my treasured and precious life.
I want to perceive,
forevermore,
the Cosmic Life
that is at my core.

73

Time is spiriting my life away.
I bow to its ceaseless march.
I knew when I came
that the name of the game
was impermanent brevity.
I have tried to live my life fully.
I have had my marvelous time.
I now yield to the rules
of the miraculous Force
that brought me here
and held me here,
just for a time,
in the Sea of the Great Divine.

74

I try to see my consciousness
but there seems to be nothing there.
Beneath the thoughts
that come and go,
that take my attention,
that pre-occupy my mind,
there is an invisible Field of Life.
I try to see Being too
but there seems to be nothing there.
Beneath the forms my eyes can see
there is an invisible Field of Life.
I realize that I carry
in my head and in my world
the miracle of Cosmic Life,
Being Itself,
in a pool in my head,
loaned to me as an act of Grace
for just this little while.

75

I see the world
as I saw my mother
in the crucial, formative
first years of life.
I am a construction formed then,
a gerrymandered complex
of perceptions,
and strategies,
and defenses,
and attitudes
and conclusions about life,
and conclusions about other people,
that were formed
before I could walk and talk.
I live through the lens
of these remnants.
I see the world through them now.
This is my constructed self
that binds me and keeps me in place.
This is the self
I must move beyond
to taste the nectar
of miraculous Cosmic Life.

76

I am coming together.
I feel it in my bones.
Something has released me,
and possessed me,
in these final stages
of the game.
I have spent decades in waiting,
blocked,
in suspended animation,
yearning for Spirit,
waiting for Spirit,
but having not a clue
about how to touch It
or what to do.
Now,
standing on the shoulders
of those who have gone before,
I am expanding
and metamorphosing.
My soul is reaching for More.

77

We must slow down
and savor the moment
for Reality to appear,
not the forms that I see
in the world before me,
but the Life beneath the appearance.
We cannot perceive the Radiance.
We cannot take part in the dance
of the infinite Matrix of Splendor
if we are spinning and whirling in place.
Slow down and open your eyes,
and open your body too.
You are planted inside
a miraculous Field
that's waiting there just for you.
It's blooming Its way
through the Cosmos,
metamorphosing constantly,
unfolding Its boundless gifts
ever-fresh and eternally new.